NORTH CAROLINA
STATE BOARD OF COMMUNITY COL
LIBRARIES
SOUTHEASTERN COMMUNITY COLLEGE

P9-CND-796

Easter

Dianne M. MacMillan

Reading Consultant:

Michael P. French, Ph.D.
Bowling Green State University

—Best Holiday Books—

ENSLOW PUBLISHERS, INC.

Bloy St. & Ramsey Ave.   P. O. Box 38
Box 777   Aldershot
Hillside, N.J. 07205   Hants GU12 6BP
U.S.A.   U.K.

For my mother, Dee

Library of Congress Cataloging-in-Publication Data

MacMillan, Dianne.
    Easter / Dianne M. MacMillan.
       p.cm. — (Best holiday books)
    Includes index.
    Summary: An introduction to the religious and secular history,
traditions, and celebrations of Easter.
    ISBN 0-89490-405-1
    1. Easter—Juvenile literature. [1. Easter.] I. Title.
II. Series.
GT4935.M33 1993
394.2'68282—dc20   92-18970
                                                  CIP
                                                      AC

Printed in the United States of America

10 9 8 7 6 5 4 3 2 1

Illustration Credits:
AP/Wide World Photos, pp. 38, 43; City of Placentia Recreation and Human Services,
pp. 28, 32; Dianne M. MacMillan, pp. 34, 44; Ester Burkholdere, p. 18; ©1992 Forest
Nicholas, p. 23; Los Angeles County Museum of Art, pp. 8, 17; Mariano Advertising,
p. 15; Mrs. Kevin Scheibel, pp. 4, 7, 12, 20, 26, 31; ©White House Historical
Association; photograph by the National Geographical Society, p. 40; Willma Willis
Gore, p. 25.

Cover Illustration:
Charlott Nathan

Contents

13.16

Families look for pretty Easter baskets on Easter Sunday morning.

Easter Sunday

It is Sunday morning. But this Sunday is different. Today is Easter. Boys and girls wake up early. They want to see what the Easter Bunny brought. The whole family gathers around the pretty Easter baskets. The baskets may be filled with colored eggs, jelly beans, or chocolate bunnies.

Many Christian families get dressed for church. Boys and girls may wear their best clothes. A girl might have a pretty dress. A boy might be wearing a dress shirt or pants. Everyone wants to look their best.

Churches are decorated with flowers and banners. Bells ring. Trumpets may sound. Choirs sing. Organs play beautiful hymns.

Everywhere there is joyful music. People sing, "Alleluia." This means "praise the Lord." The minister tells everyone that Jesus rose from the dead on Easter Sunday.

After church, families gather together. This is a special time. There is often a big Easter dinner. The table is filled with favorite foods. Some families have ham for Easter. Some families serve turkey. Others serve whatever is special for them. Sometimes there are Easter cakes and breads. The cakes may be shaped like rabbits or lambs. Some of the Easter breads have hard-boiled eggs baked inside of them. But children like the baskets of colored eggs or chocolate candy best.

If the weather is warm, boys and girls will have egg hunts or egg-rolling contests. The day is filled with fun, family, and friends.

People who believe that Jesus is the son of God are called Christians. They believe that Jesus died and came back to life and that he rose from the dead on Easter Sunday. Every spring Christians around the world celebrate Easter. For Christians, this holiday is the holiest day of the year. Easter is the oldest Christian holiday.

Churches are decorated with flowers and banners on Easter Sunday.

Jesus was nailed to a cross and died.

How Easter Began

People have celebrated the coming of spring for thousands of years. In Britain people believed that there was a goddess of spring. Her name was Eostre (A-os-tra). They believed that Eostre brought the warm sun back after winter. Our word for Easter comes from the name of the goddess.

Even though there were spring celebrations the holiday of Easter began with the death of Jesus. Jesus was born about two thousand years ago. He was Jewish and lived in Judea, which is a part of the country of Israel today. Judea was under the rule of Rome back then. Jesus began to preach when he was about thirty years old. He told all who would listen about a different way of life. He spoke about the Kingdom of God. Some of the Jewish leaders did not trust Jesus. They were afraid he would change the way things had always been done. They asked the Roman soldiers to arrest him. The Jewish leaders told the soldiers that Jesus wanted to be king of the Jews. The Romans didn't want Jesus to be a king. They thought that was wrong. Sometimes the punishment for doing something very wrong was being nailed to a cross. Jesus was nailed to a cross and died.

Jesus died on a Friday and was buried in a tomb. The tomb was carved out of a rock. A large stone was placed in front of the opening. Soldiers stood guard. On Sunday morning, his followers went to the tomb. The stone had been rolled away. The tomb was empty. They believed Jesus had risen from the dead. Jesus had said he would do this. He told people that if they believed in him, they would also be saved from death. This meant that even though a person died, he or she would come back to life, or rise again. They would live with Jesus in heaven. On Easter Sunday Christians celebrate Jesus' new life after death. They also celebrate their hope to share that new life with Jesus.

Easter falls on a different date each year. A long time ago church leaders picked a time for Easter. They decided that Easter would take place on the first Sunday after the first full moon after March 21. This means that Easter can be on a Sunday anytime between March 22 and April 25.

This girl is praying in church. For many Christians Easter is the holiest day of the year.

The Easter Season

Christians get ready for Easter for forty days. This time of getting ready is called Lent. Many people used to fast during Lent. Fasting means eating no food or eating only small amounts of food. For hundreds of years, Christians did not eat meat, cheese, eggs, and butter during Lent. Today most Christians do not give up all these foods. Some do not eat meat on Fridays. Others give up a certain food like candy or sweets. Many times children give up something they like to do like playing video games.

There are many other ways that Christians get ready for Easter. Some pray more. Some give to the poor. Others try to do special acts of kindness. Another way is to think about the wrong things they have done. They are sorry and ask God to forgive them. They will try to do better.

Lent always starts on a Wednesday. The day before Lent is called Shrove Tuesday. A long time ago it was the day for people to go to church and tell what wrongs they had done. Other people called it Pancake Tuesday. During Lent they could not eat eggs, butter, and milk. So on Pancake Tuesday they made stacks and stacks of pancakes. They stopped cooking when all of the eggs, butter, and milk were gone.

The Tuesday before Lent is called Mardi Gras. This means "fat Tuesday." This came from the French people. On this day many, many years ago they paraded a fat ox down the street. In 1704 the French people brought "fat Tuesday" to our country. They had parties and parades. The most famous Mardi Gras celebration in the United States takes place in New Orleans, Louisiana. It began in 1827. People wear costumes and masks. Bands play music. There is dancing and singing. Each year someone is chosen to be king. He is called Rex.

The next day is Ash Wednesday. Ash Wednesday is the first day of Lent. A long time ago, kings would cover their heads with ashes. This was a sign that they were sorry for anything wrong that they had done. Many Christians go to church on Ash Wednesday. In

The Mardi Gras celebration in New Orleans, Louisiana began in 1827. Many people take part in this famous parade.

some churches a priest dips his thumb into a bowl of ashes. Then he puts some ash on each person's forehead.

The last week of Lent is called Holy Week. Christians remember the things that happened to Jesus the last week before his death. Holy week begins with Palm Sunday. Jesus rode into the city of Jerusalem on this day. People spread branches of palm trees and olive trees on the ground in front of him. Others waved palm branches as he passed. Both of these actions were a sign of honor. Many churches give out palm branches on Palm Sunday because of this.

Thursday of Holy week is called Maundy Thursday (Holy Thursday). Maundy comes from an old word that means to command. Jesus commanded his followers to love one another on this night. They met together and ate supper. It is called the Last Supper because it was Jesus' last meal. After the meal was finished, Jesus went out to the garden to pray. While he was there he was arrested and taken away. Many artists have painted pictures of the Last Supper.

The next day is called Good Friday. Jesus was nailed to a cross on this day. Christians use a cross as a sign of their faith. Jesus hung on the cross until he died. He was taken down and buried. Some feel that the words "Good Friday" really mean "God's Friday."

Many churches have sunrise services on Easter Sunday. People celebrate with the first

Many artists have painted pictures of the Last Supper.

This Hollywood Bowl Easter Sunrise Service took place in 1921.
Thousands of people attend outdoor sunrise services on Easter morning.

rays of the morning sun. A folk tale from a long time ago said that on Easter morning the sun came up dancing in the sky. People would climb a high hill while it was dark. They wanted to see the sun dance. At the first sight of the sun, people sang and prayed. Bells rang. These dawn celebrations led to our Easter sunrise services. Each year thousands of people attend these outdoor services. Whether it is outside at dawn or inside a building, this is the one day when most Christians attend church.

Dyeing Easter eggs is a fun part of Easter.

Easter Eggs and Easter Baskets

There are many symbols for Easter. A symbol is something that stands for an idea. Eggs are a symbol of Easter. They stand for new life. Eggs were very valuable long before Easter became a holiday. Eggs were often dyed and given as gifts. In 1290, King Edward I had 450 eggs dyed. Then he gave one to each of his servants.

Dyeing Easter eggs is a fun part of Easter. Even people who are not Christian like to dye Easter eggs.

First the eggs are cooked in boiling water. When they are cool, they are colored with food coloring. Easter colors are purple, pink, light green, red, and pale yellow. A long time ago the yellow color stood for the returning sun. Red stood for joy and life.

Dyeing eggs is an art form in some countries. In Poland and Ukraine, eggs are painted with many designs and colors. Polish eggs are called "pysanki" (pee-SANK-ee). Pysanki means eggs with lines on them. A special pen is used. Designs are made by putting lines of wax on an egg. Then the egg is dipped in dye. The wax lines keep that part of the egg from changing colors. Then more lines are added. The egg is dipped in dye again. This is repeated a few more times. Finally the wax is melted off the egg. Pysanki eggs may take six or seven hours to make. Some can take several days to make. Each egg is different. But they are all beautiful to look at. People give the eggs as gifts. Some families have pysanki eggs that were dyed over 100 years ago.

Some German Americans in Pennsylvania scratch designs on eggs. They use a sharp needle on dyed eggs. They scratch pictures of

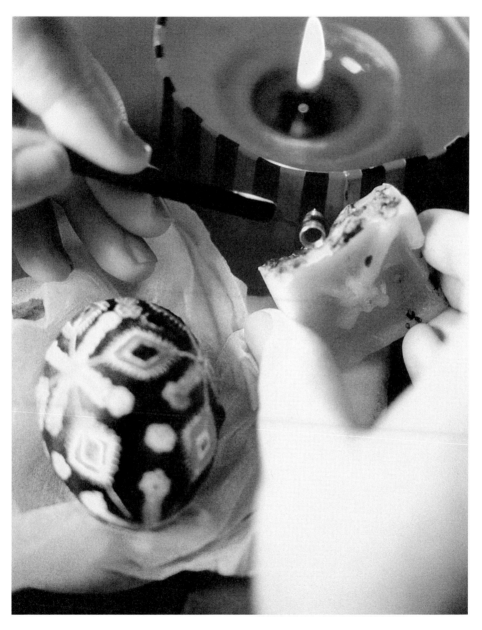

Pysanki eggs are painted with many designs and colors.

hearts, tulips, and butterflies. This folk art is handed down from one family member to another.

Some families like to make Easter egg trees. First they make a tiny hole on both ends of an egg. Then they blow the insides of the egg out from one end. The egg shells are then dyed or painted. Ribbons are glued to one end when the shells are dry. The eggs are hung on branches of a small tree.

In the 1890s a Russian by the name of Peter Carl Fabergé (fa-ber-JAY) made eggs out of gold, silver, and jewels. The kings and other rulers wanted Fabergé Easter eggs. Some of the eggs opened up. There were tiny carvings of people or animals inside. Today some of these beautiful eggs can be seen in museums.

The first Easter baskets were not really baskets. They looked more like bird nests. They were made from grass. They were placed on the ground or in the barn. Sometimes a boy's or girl's hat was filled with straw. Later, baskets

Some people collect eggs decorated in the Fabergé-style.

Easter baskets like this one may contain colored eggs and gifts.

were filled with straw. Today Easter baskets are decorated with ribbons and flowers. They have real or fake straw. They can be filled with chocolate candy, jelly beans, decorated eggs, or small gifts.

The Easter bunny is a favorite symbol of Easter.

Easter Bunny

Children look forward to Easter morning. They are hoping to find an Easter basket filled with candy or eggs. Some children think it is the Easter Bunny who brings the eggs. The Easter Bunny is another favorite symbol of Easter. No one knows how the legend of the Easter Bunny bringing eggs began. A legend is a story that is told from year to year. Many people believe in legends even though they are not always true.

The goddess Eostre always had a hare with her. A hare is like a rabbit, but it is larger. The hare was a symbol of the moon.

It also stood for the rebirth of nature. Rabbits and hares have many babies in a year. Because of this they are a symbol of new life. In later years people used the rabbit as a symbol of Easter instead of the larger hare.

One story about the Easter Bunny tells of a poor lady. She did not have any money to buy gifts for her children. All she had were some eggs. She dyed the eggs. Then she hid them in her garden. Afterwards, she told the children to go look for their surprises. While the children were searching, a rabbit hopped out from under a bush. The children said the bunny brought them some eggs. They called it the Easter Bunny because he brought the eggs at Easter.

Another story tells about a German duchess. Every year she dyed eggs for the children. Then she would hide them. She told the children that the Easter Bunny hid them.

There are many customs about the hare or rabbit. A custom is something that is done over and over again. Many customs have come from German people who came to America a long time ago. In one custom, children built nests for the rabbit before Easter. They hid the nests in the barn and around the house. The children believed that if they were good, the rabbit would lay Easter eggs in the nest.

Another custom began in Texas in 1846. On the night before Easter the people built bonfires.

Some Easter Sundays are snowy, but everyone still likes to think about the Easter Bunny.

Children like to do things with an Easter Bunny. These children are winners of an egg hunt.

They told the children that the fires were made by the Easter Bunny. He was making his dyes for the Easter eggs by burning wild flowers.

During the Easter season, there are Easter Bunnies in stores. Children can have their pictures taken with a big Easter Bunny. There are stories, songs, and books about the Easter Bunny.

The Easter lily was brought to the United States from the country of
Bermuda in 1880.

Easter Clothes and Plants

Another Easter custom is wearing new clothes. A long time ago the new year began in March. People wore new clothes to show they were making a new beginning. Early Christians were baptized and joined the church on Easter. They wore white robes to show they were starting a new life. This is how a legend began. Anyone who was wearing something new on Easter would have good luck for the next year. It did not have to cost a lot of money, as long as it was new. Even poor people tried to wear something new. It might be a new scarf, or ribbon, or shoe laces.

Later on girls and women wore a new hat or bonnet on Easter. A legend said that if a girl wore a new hat or bonnet on Easter, she would find happiness and love in the new year.

Everyone enjoys the first sign of spring flowers. Crocuses, daffodils, and tulips bloom almost everywhere. Women wear flowers pinned to their dresses on Easter Sunday. Flowers are used to decorate churches and homes.

The flower of Easter is a kind of lily. It has big white blossoms. They are shaped like bells. The lily has a very sweet smell. Churches are filled with lilies on Easter Sunday. Many people give these plants as gifts. This type of lily first came from Bermuda. A lady from the United States visited there in 1880. She thought the lilies were beautiful. She was surprised because the lilies were blooming in March. The lilies that grew in the United States bloomed much later in the summer. She brought the Bermuda lily plants back to Philadelphia. Soon everyone wanted one. They were named the Easter lily.

Getting Ready for Easter

Boys and girls like to make things for Easter. You can make baskets from colored paper. Sometimes you can cut baskets from milk cartons. Then they are decorated. Each child dyes an egg to put inside when the basket is finished. Sometimes the eggs are colored with markers.

It is fun to paint pictures of the Easter Bunny. Cotton is glued on for the rabbit's tail. Small children cut out pink bunny ears to wear. Everyone likes to read stories and poems about spring and Easter.

In some classrooms there is an Easter bonnet contest. Whoever comes to school with the craziest hat wins. Other classes make Easter

This girl's hat won first prize in an Easter bonnet contest in Florida.

hats out of paper plates. Children glue flowers, leaves, and anything else a person can think of on top. Then everyone parades around the school.

A few months before Easter, people plant flower seeds. When the plant is grown it will be an Easter gift. Some children make Easter cards with yarn and ribbon for their parents. They decorate the cards with Easter symbols.

A girl gives the Easter Bunny a hug during the annual White House Easter Egg Roll.

Things to Do on Easter

Children all over the world like to hunt for Easter eggs. Sometimes there are egg hunts in parks. Most children hunt for eggs in their back yards or homes. It is fun to see who can find the most eggs.

Egg rolling is a game that children used to play a long time ago. In 1809, President James Madison's wife, Dolly Madison, invited children to the lawn by the Capitol building. The children rolled eggs down the hill. The egg that reached the bottom first won a prize.

President Rutherford B. Hayes moved the party to the south lawn of the White House in the 1870s. It is still held there each year on Easter Monday.

Easter parades are fun to walk in. Towns all over the United States and Canada have these parades. Many years ago men and women walked around after church. They wanted to show off their new clothes. A person with a candle walked ahead of them. This walking later became the Easter parades we have today. There are prizes for the best dressed person and for the prettiest hat.

The most famous parade is in New York City. It began in 1850. In the beginning only very rich people were in the parade. They rode in grand carriages. Everyone wore beautiful new clothes. Today the streets are closed so there is no traffic. Anyone can walk down Fifth Avenue. Some people even dress up their dogs and cats and bring them along. Everyone has a good time greeting one another.

Some people like to send Easter cards. Many cards have Easter Symbols like a lily or a cross on them. Some show the Easter Bunny with baskets of eggs. Other cards show baby animals.

Chicks, ducklings, bunnies, and lambs are symbols of new life and Easter. People also like to give Easter gifts. Some gifts they give are candy or Easter lilies.

In some parts of our country Good Friday and Easter Monday are holidays. Banks and businesses are closed. Most schools are closed the week before Easter or the week after. School

These people are celebrating at the New York Easter parade.

children look forward to the Easter vacation. Some people call this the spring break from school.

Easter is a joyful holiday for young and old. It is a time for family and friends. It is not just a Christian holiday. Anyone can celebrate the joy of the spring, the rebirth of nature, and the blessings of the new year.

Easter is a fun holiday for family and friends.

Glossary

baptize—To make a person a member of a Christian church by dipping him/her in water or sprinkling him/her with water.

Christians—People who believe that Jesus is the son of God.

command—To order something be done. On Maundy Thursday Jesus commanded his followers to love one another.

custom—Something that is done over and over.

Eostre—A goddess of spring.

fast—To not eat food or eat only small amounts of food.

heaven—The place where Christians believe God and the angels live. Christians believe they will share this life with Jesus after they die.

legend—A story that is told over and over again before it is written down. It may or may not be true.

Last Supper—The last meal that Jesus ate before his death.

Lent—A time of preparing for Easter.

maundy—An old word that means to command.

pysanki—Polish eggs decorated with many lines and colors.

symbol—Something that stands for an idea or for something else.

Index
